HEADS
OF
STATE

HEAD

S

CARL SFERRAZZA ANTHONY

OF STATE

A FAIR STREET BOOK

BLOOMSBURY

Dedication:
To My Funny Friends: Jeff "Magic Baker" Buhler, Robert "Father of Grace" Campbell,
Patti "The Pirate" Cullen, James "BMW" Fuller, Rich "Future Plastics" Gottwald,
Joe "Get the Music" Guthrie, Nancee "Sacre Bleu" Hacskaylo, Jim "Geo" Harden,
Kurt "Stirring the Pot" Hessler, Rebecca "Grumplicia" Hughes, Karen "Samurai Sister" Lowe,
John "cc: Esq." McGuire, Peter "Sun King" McManus, Morgan "Superman" Molthrop,
Claire "Mrs. Swifty" Sanders and, of course, Rich "Oh! Witty One!" Sullivan

Text Copyright © 2004 by Carl Sferrazza Anthony
Compilation © 2004 Fair Street Productions

Produced by Fair Street Productions, New York
Deborah Bull & Susan Wechsler, Directors

Designer: Jon Glick / mouse+tiger, New York
Photographer: Steven Mays, New York

Published by Bloomsbury, New York and London
Distributed to the trade by Holtzbrinck Publishers

All papers used by Bloomsbury are natural, recyclable products made from wood grown in
well-managed forests. The manufacturing processes conform to the environmental
regulations of the country of origin.

Library of Congress Cataloging-in-Publication Data

Anthony, Carl Sferrazza.
Heads of state / Carl Sferrazza Anthony.—1st U.S. ed.
p. cm.
ISBN 1-58234-512-0 (hc.)
1. Presidents—Collectibles—United States. 2. Presidents—United States—Portraits. 3. Americana.
4. Souvenirs (Keepsakes)—United States. 5. Political Collectibles—United States. 6. Material culture—
United States. 7. Popular culture—United States. I. Title.

E176.1.A69 2004
973'.092'2—dc22
2004049678

First U.S. Edition 2004

1 3 5 7 9 10 8 6 4 2

Printed by C&C Offset Printing Company Ltd., China

Also by Carl Sferrazza Anthony

This Elevated Position... A Guide to the National First Ladies Library and Introduction to First Ladies History

America's Most Influential First Ladies

The Kennedy White House: Family Life and Pictures, 1961-1963

America's First Families: An Inside View of Two Hundred Years of Private Life in the White House

Florence Harding: The First Lady, The Jazz Age and the Death of America's Most Scandalous President

As We Remember Her: Jacqueline Kennedy Onassis in the Words of Her Friends and Family

First Ladies: The Saga of the Presidents' Wives and Their Power, 1789-1990 (two volumes)

TABLE OF CONTENTS

INTRODUCTION

WHETHER IT WAS FOUR-TERM FRANKLIN D. ROOSEVELT or one-term Franklin Pierce, the presidents have always been America's ultimate celebrities—famous, powerful, and (even if only as a guy with keys to the Treasury) wealthy. Since the first days of the presidency in the spring of 1789, the names and faces of the presidents have been instantly recognizable to almost every citizen—even those who couldn't read or speak English. And since the new nation was a democracy and the leader was not a sacred king, the president could be lampooned in the press, libeled by his rivals, and thrown out of his public housing by the people. Under American democracy, a ruler's head could still find its way onto a platter—but only figuratively, as part of a commemorative set from the Franklin Mint.

Right from the start, American enterprise literally saw a good thing in the face of the chief executive, commercially manufacturing and ingeniously marketing it as various household products. Who could resist (or forget) the great Thomas Jefferson staring at you with some daisies in his head? Or James Polk on a cigar label? Or Grover Cleveland decorating a seltzer bottle?

In the earliest administrations, printed engravings of the presidents' faces on thick wood-pulp paper were hot sellers in printing and newspaper shops. These presidential images soon were printed on a lighter paper that transferred to ceramic objects. This so-called "transferware" of blue- or black-ink images on cream-colored ceramics served unique political purposes: A pitcher calling for bipartisanship featured Federalist John Adams on one side and anti-Federalist James Madison on the other, with a poem beseeching them to get along.

What best cleaned up the spill from a James Monroe coffee mug or cracked Thomas Jefferson jug? An Andrew Jackson handkerchief, of course! Handkerchiefs depicting George Washington had been made during the American Revolution, but soon enough Jefferson and other presidents were crudely printed on cloth banners, scarves, and ribbons. They became the second "rage" of presidential head images on commercial products. And it wasn't long before campaign managers recognized a good thing.

By the time the son of John Adams—John Quincy Adams—ran against the popular military hero Andrew Jackson in 1824, the transfer images were no longer made from engravings but from prints of the candidates' portrait paintings. They were then pasted or shellacked onto other items—a John Quincy Adams sewing box or an Andrew Jackson or Martin Van Buren snuffbox.

During the 1841 campaign of William Henry Harrison, the first Whig candidate, a wider variety of objects depicting the candidate—gravy boats, china plates, glass log cabins, sheet music, and even paper stationery—flooded the market. By the next election in 1844, Democrat James Polk appeared on wallpaper and even on a quilt.

"Tokens," metallic discs depicting the candidates in profile encircled by a slogan, had been popular since at least the Martin Van Buren presidency. Suggestive of ancient coins that glorified Roman emperors, they were eventually turned into buttons that could be sewn onto coats and jackets—as seen in the rare example representing Zachary Taylor, included here. Taylor was also the first presidential candidate whose image jumped from a one-dimensional object to a three-dimensional one, a clay pipe. The heads of subsequent candidates—Millard Fillmore, Franklin Pierce—were also turned into pipes.

The age of the presidential head had arrived.

A NOTE ON THE COLLECTION

AN HISTORIAN MUST TAKE HIS WORK SERIOUSLY—but his friends do not have to take him seriously. Mine certainly do not. On a June night in the mid-1990s, the perpetually irreverent sibling team of Edward and Rita Purcell first presented me with the head of a president—a John F. Kennedy bust bank—as a birthday gift. The George Washington cameo soap cake soon followed at Christmas. Subsequent celebrations brought forth more curiosity shop finds from those Purcells: an LBJ plastic doll, a Jimmy Carter peanut walking man, even a Bess Truman doll head. And so this collection of presidential heads began.

I'd always abhorred hoarding and previously had avoided any serious collecting; it had always seemed to me that what might begin in glee as a pastime often deteriorates into a humorless— let alone expensive—obsession. Still, after this distinguished gathering of plastic and plaster and so forth entered my life, I was intrigued with the idea of assembling a unique collection, unlike any other. Many presidential collections have been assembled—autographs, portraits, personal possessions, campaign buttons—but who else could say they had a different head or image of each president that was an everyday, useful household item? And soon enough I was actively pursing those presidential heads, an effort begun in earnest by 1999, fueled by the ease of eBay. *Heads of State* is the result. The only rule was that each president be useful in his own, individualistic manner.

The items in *Heads of State* represent only a fraction of the collection. There are, of course, the "also rans." I don't mean Fritz Mondale or Bob Dole or Adlai Stevenson. I mean the Taft cream pitcher, the Hoover pencil eraserhead, the Harding wooden nickel, the Kennedy charm bracelet, the Washington cake plate, and the Lincoln whistle. These other presidential head items simply did not make the cut.

Finally, I must mention that there remains an ever-elusive group of heads lurking in attics and flea market boxes. The Wilson nutcracker, the Van Buren snuff box, the Washington drawer handles, the Harding change purse, the Grant match safe, the Hayes belt buckle...I know they're out there somewhere and I vow to keep the hunt alive until they are all captured.

—Carl Sferrazza Anthony

GEORGE WASHINGTON

1ˢᵗ President ★ 1789–1797 ★ Federalist

THIMBLE

FIRST IN THE HEARTS OF HIS COUNTRYMEN, father of his country, first president of the United States—George Washington is *the* American icon. Standing six feet two inches tall in his silk stockings and silver-buckled shoes, his mere presence commanded respect.

Washington laid the framework for the new government but, above all, he personally symbolized the new, democratic America. He may have held on to some aristocratic habits—he traveled in a regal coach with servants in liveried uniforms—but the first president made it clear that he would not do any of it the British way. He would not be king.

> What sort of patriot, then, would seek to diminish this figurative and literal giant to a mere sewing thimble?

What sort of patriot, then, would seek to diminish this figurative and literal giant to a mere sewing thimble? Who would dare to so materially belittle this great man? A close inspection of the small print inside the thimble cannot tell a lie—it was made in England.

13

JOHN ADAMS

2nd President ★ **1797–1801** ★ **Federalist**

BEER CANS

SHORT, FAT, AND INTENSE, John Adams was easily overlooked between the gentlemanly Virginians Washington and Jefferson.

Always an ale man, Adams managed to enrage wine-drinking Francophiles like Jefferson. He refused to pay a bribe to three anonymous French negotiators in what became known as the "XYZ Affair," and pushed through the Alien Act that permitted the deportation of non-citizen immigrants—mostly French—who were deemed a threat during wartime.

> **Always an ale man, Adams managed to enrage wine-drinking Francophiles like Jefferson.**

Despite the fact that he played a crucial role in the drafting of the Declaration of Independence, during America's Bicentennial, it was Washington and Jefferson who got national face-time on souvenir busts, plates, and other paraphernalia. The countenance of John Adams made its way most prominently onto aluminum beer cans. It was a brand soon enough discontinued and forgotten—in contrast to that popular beer named for a fellow revolutionary, his cousin Sam.

THOMAS JEFFERSON

3ʳᵈ President ★ 1801–1809 ★ Democratic-Republican

FLOWER VASE

THOMAS JEFFERSON—EXPERT IN MUSIC, architecture, philosophy, government, and scientific invention—loved, above all, being a planter. He not only snuck a grain of rice into the United States for cultivation, but also tended to his vineyard, nurtured flower gardens, and had an eye for the beauty of the mountain views from his home. It was only natural that such a lover of the land would seek to expand his country by negotiating the Louisiana Purchase and sending the Lewis and Clark Expedition to explore the West.

> There could be no more appropriate object to feature this Renaissance president, who always planted so many ideas in his head, than a flower planter.

There could be no more appropriate object to feature this Renaissance president, who always planted so many ideas in his head, than a flower planter.

Made by the American firm Enesco during the "head planter" craze of the late 1950s and early '60s, Tall Tom was the rare male among the more usual smiling female head planters. Certainly, he would have enjoyed that.

17

JAMES MADISON

4ᵗʰ President ★ 1809–1817 ★ Democratic-Republican
WHISKEY BOTTLE

DESCRIBED BY WASHINGTON IRVING as "poor, little Jemmy," a wrinkled, small old man, James Madison's two-term presidency was dominated by the unpopular War of 1812.

His most enduring success as president was, in fact, his first lady. Dolley Madison was a justly celebrated hostess who also shaped that position into a public role.

> His most enduring success as president was, in fact, his first lady.

Her open house receptions on Wednesday were crammed full of visitors—from stiff New England congressmen in black leather shoes to Westerners in muddy boots. They socialized around her famous bowls of punch—heavily doused with whiskey, all paid for out of the personal pocket of President Madison. So, despite the fact that presidents including James Monroe, John Adams, Ulysses S. Grant, and Theodore Roosevelt have all taken the form of whiskey decanters, the honor really belongs to one man—little Jemmy.

James Madison

1809-1817

JAMES MONROE

COFFEE CUP

JAMES MONROE'S FAMOUS MONROE DOCTRINE put out the word that no nations could colonize or in any other way interfere with the countries or regions of the Western Hemisphere—from South America to Canada.

This reproduction coffee cup featuring Monroe is typical of the creamware (cream-colored pottery) made between 1789 and 1820 to honor, or promote, the first five presidents. Most of these British-manufactured items were jugs or large pitchers that featured portraits transferred from engravings. Monroe—patriotic as he was—never loomed as large a figure as Washington, Adams, or Jefferson. Somehow, he just wasn't big enough to fill a jug.

Monroe—patriotic as he was—never loomed as large a figure as Washington, Adams, or Jefferson. (Somehow, he just wasn't big enough to fill a jug.)

But considering the endless flow of coffee beans imported into the United States—undoubtedly due, in part, to his doctrine—Monroe seems just the fellow with whom to enjoy a cup of java.

21

JOHN QUINCY ADAMS

6th President ★ 1825–1829 ★ National Republican-Whig

CANDLE SNUFFER

"**I** AM A MAN OF RESERVED, COLD, AUSTERE, and forbidding manners," John Quincy Adams confessed. He was, at least, honest. More comfortable with books than with people, Adams, who was fascinated by science and technology, prompted the building of canals and turnpikes and helped establish the Smithsonian Institution. The first son of a president to get himself elected to the same position, he was unlike John Adams, his father, in that he belittled his wife's intelligence and often discouraged her offers of wise advice. JQA's presidential run flickered out after just one term.

> Dark in mood and chilly in spirit, the gloomy countenance of John Quincy Adams was stamped onto the handle of a candle snuffer...

Dark in mood and chilly in spirit, the gloomy countenance of John Quincy Adams was stamped onto the handle of a candle snuffer by silversmith W.M. Rogers. His grim demeanor could put out anyone's flame.

ANDREW JACKSON

7ᵗʰ President ★ **1829–1837** ★ **Democrat**

TABLE LAMP

UNENLIGHTENED IN HIS ATTITUDE toward Native Americans, to most Americans Andrew Jackson—the great general of the Battle of New Orleans—radiated power. His electric declaration "Our Union! It must be preserved!" struck down Southern demands for states' rights and the principal of nullification. And to Western settlers, Andrew Jackson was one of them, their first representative in the White House.

> If he wasn't exactly a beacon of hope for all, Jackson was certainly a leading light for many.

In his day Jackson appeared on handkerchiefs and plates, usually seated on his white charger bucking backward. A Democratic favorite of FDR and Harry Truman, Jackson enjoyed a posthumous revival of popularity in the 1940s, the period during which this odd table lamp was made—possibly from an Old Hickory Distilling decanter. If he wasn't exactly a beacon of hope for all, Jackson was certainly a leading light for many.

MARTIN VAN BUREN

8th President ★ 1837–1841 ★ Democrat

GOLD PLATE

MARTIN VAN BUREN IS THE MAN TO THANK for the expression, "O.K." It was his nickname, referring to "Old Kinderhook," the upstate New York village where he was born. Van Buren had political misfortunes, but his final downfall was the dining room. As Americans suffered through economic depression, Van Buren gallivanted in his silk-lined coach, wore monogrammed buckled shoes, and sought federal funds for an even more regal mansion to call home. Reports of dinners set with a "silver plate" and gold utensils prompted the famous "Gold Spoon" speech by Congressman Charles Ogle, which helped defeat Van Buren in the 1840 election.

> Van Buren had political misfortunes, but his final downfall was the dining room.

This silver and gold plate is actually one in a White House Historical Association series. But no presidential visage shines more appropriately from the set than does Van Buren's.

26

Martin Van Buren

8th President of the United States

Sold by Allen & Co. 72 State Street.

WILLIAM HENRY HARRISON

9th President ⭐ **1841-1841** ⭐ **Whig**

STATIONERY

WILLIAM HENRY HARRISON IS most notable for how he won the presidency and for how he left it.

Born and raised on a Virginia plantation, Harrison built a military and political career in the Northwest Territory. There, at Tippecanoe Creek, he led a surprise attack against Indians who had been killing settlers and became a national celebrity.

> Harrison's Democrat opponents portrayed him as a tired old farmer drinking hard cider in his log cabin.

Harrison's Democrat opponents portrayed him as a tired old farmer drinking hard cider in his log cabin. But supporters turned this to their advantage, selling him as a man of the people. Images of farm plows, cider barrels, and log cabins were rushed onto plates, banners, ribbons—and even stationery, as seen here in this rare example.

After delivering the longest inaugural speech in history during a driving rainstorm, he developed a cold and died thirty days later—certainly no president to write home about.

29

JOHN TYLER

10ᵗʰ President ★ **1841–1845** ★ **Whig**

WALL HANGING

AFTER HARRISON'S DEATH, Vice President John Tyler assumed the presidency and established the precedent of presidential succession.

Sixteen years after leaving the White House, Tyler gave his loyalty to the Confederacy, was elected to the Dixie Congress, and declared a traitor to the Union. What was left of his reputation was salvaged by the fact that he met his maker before he could actually serve in the Confederate government.

> ...he met his maker before he could actually serve in the Confederate government.

Moments after his death, plaster was applied to his face and a mold of his features was made. The death mask here is one of several copies cast from the original. This one is especially peculiar because it was made with a hook in the back, for display on the parlor wall.

Even if Tyler's head were never hung in shame, one would have to be a fairly morbid rebel to hang it as decor.

30

JAMES POLK

11ᵗʰ President ★ **1845–1849** ★ **Democrat**

CIGAR BAND

JAMES POLK USED THE POPULAR CONCEPT OF Manifest Destiny to expand the continental United States, suggesting that it was God's will that America stretch from sea to shining sea.

Whether Polk believed this is hard to determine. All he said and did was calculated for political success. With his obsessive penchant for work and disdain of wasted time, Polk's sole social indulgence was escorting his overbearing wife, Sarah, to her Presbyterian church. Only on those Sundays when she stayed at home did Polk attend services in his preferred faith of Methodism. And only on his deathbed did he finally defy Sarah, refusing baptism from her minister and summoning a Methodist one instead.

That Polk's face appears on a cigar band is highly ironic. Sarah outlawed all hard alcohol, card playing, dancing, and even music in the White House, but smoking tobacco was the one vice she failed to forbid.

> Polk's sole social indulgence was escorting his overbearing wife, Sarah, to her Presbyterian church.

33

ZACHARY TAYLOR

12ᵗʰ President ★ **1849–1850** ★ **Whig**

COAT BUTTON

"**N**EVER JUDGE A STRANGER BY HIS CLOTHES," said Zachary Taylor, who lived up to his motto. The legendary "Old Rough and Ready" led America to victory in the Mexican War, but he was frequently mistaken for an old farmer on his way to market.

His lack of pretension applied to politics, too. Notified that the Whigs had nominated him as president via a postage due letter, Taylor refused to pay. Despite being a slaveholder, Taylor did not want slavery extended into the new territories.

Taylor's 1848 Whig campaign repeated some of the gimmickry of the 1840 one: "Rough and Ready" appeared on snuffboxes, ribbons, and scarves. But that year his profile was also minted in relief onto brass buttons for a gentleman's topcoat. Today a rare collectible, it was about as close to a fancy coat as he ever got.

> The legendary "Old Rough and Ready" led America to victory in the Mexican War, but he was frequently mistaken for an old farmer on his way to market.

MILLARD FILLMORE

13ᵗʰ President ★ **1850–1853** ★ **Whig**

PIPE

MILLARD FILLMORE. HIS VERY NAME is synonymous with obscurity, perhaps rightly so. He signed the Fugitive Slave Bill that allowed Southern slaveholders to pursue and capture their runaway slaves in free territory, and later ran for president on an anti-Catholic ticket.

No wonder Fillmore is best known for installing the first White House library and stove. The persistent tale that he also installed the first White House bathtub is not true, but he was hailed as a specimen of the healthy, outdoor pioneer life—the hearty sort who could endure a regular cold bath in the tubs already in place at the executive mansion. Not surprisingly, he did not smoke; soap bubbles were the only thing he would have blown out of this 1856 clay pipe bowl of himself. And he thought he could get back to the White House for a second term, but he was blowing pipe dreams.

> **Fillmore is best known for installing the first White House library and stove.**

36

FRANKLIN PIERCE

14ᵗʰ President ★ 1853–1857 ★ Democrat

SUSPENDER CLIP

CAMPAIGN SOUVENIRS HIT AN ALL-TIME LOW when it was decided that a suspender clip to keep trousers up was just the place to put the face of Franklin Pierce.

Pierce was unhappy in private: He had an alcoholic mother, a severely depressed wife, and three young sons who all died before maturity.

> Pierce had certainly done little to hold the Union together, and nothing to lift the atmosphere of impending doom.

His political life seemed to match his personal one, most notably the bloody riots that tore through Kansas as the debate over slavery intensified. It was remarkable that the nation did not then plunge into sectional warfare. Pierce had certainly done little to hold the Union together, and nothing to lift the atmosphere of impending doom. In fact, by the end of his term, it was abundantly clear that suspenders were about the only thing he could keep raised.

39

JAMES BUCHANAN

15th President ★ **1857–1861** ★ **Democrat**

TOOTHPICK HOLDER

J AMES BUCHANAN'S ACCOMPLISHMENTS could easily fit into the toothpick holder that represents him here, made in Italy sixty years after his administration.

Too small a statesman to stem the onset of civil war, Buchanan did nothing to prevent the secession of the Southern states. But he was the ultimate gentleman who would be perfectly at place at a soirée. As president, his greatest achievements were probably ceremonial: He was the first president to host a foreign dignitary as an overnight guest in the White House—Edward, Prince of Wales. Stiffly fastidious in dress and manner, Buchanan served haute cuisine to his guests and drove about in a grand carriage. He may have done nothing to prevent the sectional tensions that led to the Civil War, but he threw some really great parties.

> **He may have done nothing to prevent the sectional tensions that led to the Civil War, but he threw some really great parties.**

BUCHANAN

ABRAHAM LINCOLN

16ᵗʰ President ★ 1861–1865 ★ Republican

PAPER CLIP

IF HE COULD GUIDE A NATION through its most unstable period, imagine how well Abraham Lincoln could turn a messy desk of papers into a tidy bundle. Given the dark times of his administration, as well as his assassination, Lincoln's image has generally been appropriated for honorable items, such as solemn wall plaques and bookends. The heavy brass office clasp shown here is really an early form of a large paperclip that dates from the late nineteenth century— a sentimental, practical object for the workplace.

> ...imagine how well Abraham Lincoln could turn a messy desk of papers into a tidy bundle.

Lincoln was aided by a well-organized executive staff, and the current "Lincoln bedroom" at the White House was actually his office. One would not want to suggest that brass office clasps won the war for Lincoln, but even the Great Emancipator certainly used all the help he could get.

43

ANDREW JOHNSON

17ᵗʰ President ★ **1865–1869** ★ **Unionist Democrat**

DRINK COASTER

FEW PRESIDENTS HAVE BEEN MORE HUMILIATED than Andrew Johnson. During the Civil War he was despised as a traitor in much of his native South, and afterward he was hated by many Northerners for his relatively gentle Reconstruction policy. All sides were quick to recall the lingering story of his intoxication at his swearing-in ceremony as vice president—an incident attributed to illness. The final result of it all? Johnson became the first U.S. president to be impeached—though he was not removed from office.

Originally a tailor, he learned to read and write late in life. Yet he didn't even have the satisfaction of being memorialized on a pair of shears or a coat or shirt. No, he was just a drink coaster, there to absorb the run-off.

> All sides were quick to recall the lingering story of his intoxication at his swearing-in ceremony as vice president...

44

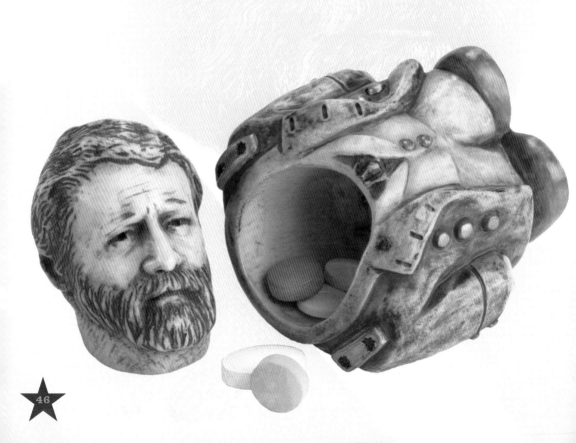

ULYSSES S. GRANT

18ᵗʰ President ★ **1869–1877** ★ **Republican**

PILL BOX

A GREAT GENERAL, ULYSSES S. GRANT was hailed as the savior of the Union.

He had never lusted for the presidency, and there is much evidence to suggest that he pursued it at the urging of his wife, Julia. He sought to protect the constitutional rights recently given to freed slaves, but politically naïve, Grant was duped by many that he trusted and his presidency was riddled with scandal.

…Grant, even in his Union uniform, appears a tiny man.

Depicted in a contemporary resin pill box made by the Harmony Ball Company, the famed military leader Grant, even in his Union uniform, appears a tiny man. In the years following his administration, very little could boost his diminished stature. And well over a century later, one still gets a sense that Julia Grant could still be…well, a bit of a pill.

47

RUTHERFORD B. HAYES

19th President ★ 1877–1881 ★ Republican

GOLF BALL

FOR A GOOD SCOTSMAN who enjoyed lawn tennis and croquet, it seemed natural that Rutherford B. Hayes would have been the first president to take up that most presidential of sports—golf. But he didn't.

Taking office under charges of election fraud, Hayes had some of the bitterness directed at him sweetened by his wife, Lucy. She began the custom of formally inviting children to come roll hard, round objects on the South Lawn of the White House for an official Easter Egg Roll.

When Hayes withdrew the last federal troops from the South—placed there during Reconstruction—he had not intended for white supremacists to brutalize blacks into second-class citizenship. He may not have been figuratively on the ball then, but at least he is literally on it now.

> He may not have been figuratively on the ball then, but at least he is literally on it now.

48

JAMES GARFIELD

20th President ★ **1881-1881** ★ **Republican**

TRIVET

THE HOT-TEMPERED JAMES GARFIELD rose from a humble background, helping his widowed mother keep the farm by working as a canal boy. Somewhat intense and touchy-feely for a Victorian, he was a man who hugged easily and liked to put his arm around another's shoulder. Always a passionate person, he used considerable effort to cool his emotions. And thus this heavy iron Garfield kitchen trivet, used to cool off hot pans and plates, is just the right fit.

> Somewhat intense and touchy-feely for a Victorian, he was a man who hugged easily and liked to put his arm around another's shoulder.

Garfield's image was often tied to food. When he ran for president, boxed sweets featuring his face were sold as "Our Candy Date." A certain blend of herbal tea—dubbed "Garfield Tea"—stimulated good digestion. After his assassination, Garfield even appeared on clear glass dinner plates, beer steins, and coffee mugs, machine-pressed in Industrial Age factories for a grieving public.

CHESTER A. ARTHUR

21ˢᵗ President ★ **1881–1885** ★ **Republican**

DOORSTOP

THOSE WHO THOUGHT Chester A. Arthur paid too much attention to his fancy clothes and not enough to giving his pals good jobs nicknamed him "The Dude." But if politicos with palms itchy for Gilded Age graft were dumbstruck at the honesty of Arthur, less powerful citizens were delighted; former collector of the Port of New York, Arthur enacted sweeping civil service reform.

There may seem to be an endless number of useless purposes for a weighty iron commemorative bust (made in the 1970s by the Franklin Mint). But considering all those citizens for whom he first held open the door of employment, this small but firm Chester Arthur is really the perfect doorstop: He put a halt to patronage and let qualified, regular folks in for government jobs.

> ...this small but firm Chester Arthur is really the perfect doorstop...

52

GROVER CLEVELAND

22ⁿᵈ/24ᵗʰ President ★ **1885–1889/1893-1897** ★ **Democrat**

SELTZER BOTTLE

THE SECOND FATTEST PRESIDENT (William Taft was the fattest), Grover Cleveland, ate breakfasts that included oatmeal, mutton chops, eggs, and coffee. Instead of gourmet meals, he preferred pickled herring, Swiss cheese, and a chop, and his favorite dish was corned beef and cabbage. Inevitably, indigestion came next, and then relief from "charged water."

The presidency upset Cleveland's stomach, too.

The presidency upset Cleveland's stomach, too. During his campaigns, he was accused of everything from fathering an illegitimate child to "beer-swilling." Fighting with labor interests over tariffs and battling with veterans over pensions, he lost re-election. A glutton for punishment, he ran again four years later and won, only to be plagued by rioting railroad strikers and an economic depression. Any wonder he had acute indigestion, relieved by a stomach pump? Imbibing from the seltzer bottle would have been a lot easier.

BENJAMIN HARRISON

23ʳᵈ President ★ **1889–1893** ★ **Republican**

TIE PIN

BENJAMIN HARRISON COULD NOT HELP leaving a lingering sense of smallness. Gifted at making spontaneous speeches, he always delivered them in a soft voice. Running on the campaign slogan of "Rejuvenated Republicanism," his tenure, confessed a G.O.P. Senate wife, was as "conventional as a sideboard."

At five feet six inches tall, he was soon enough dubbed "Little Ben."

Tariff protectionist, defender of veteran pensions—perhaps Harrison's greatest claim to fame was the fact that he was the grandson of the ninth president, William Henry Harrison. At five feet six inches tall, he was soon enough dubbed "Little Ben." Cartoons invariably showed him being swallowed up by the oversized beaver hat of his legendary ancestor.

Perhaps it was a mean little pinch, but the year he ran for president, Harrison was represented by a tiny gold tie pin—the smallest presidential head, in fact, in *Heads of State*.

WILLIAM McKINLEY

25ᵗʰ President ★ 1897–1901 ★ Republican

CANE TOP

DURING THE FRENCH REVOLUTION, heads of noblemen were mounted on sticks. A century later in Canton, Ohio, the head of native son William McKinley was turned into brass, mass-produced, and placed atop canes. Fashionable walking sticks topped with presidential heads had appeared as early as Thomas Jefferson, but McKinley was one of the last chief executives so honored.

> Although McKinley personally conducted himself honestly, some of his brass may not have.

Although McKinley personally conducted himself honestly, some of his brass may not have. On his watch, the Spanish-American War began when the U.S. battleship *Maine* was sunk in Havana Harbor. McKinley declared war after being informed that the Spanish had blown up the *Maine*—but that was never proven. He may not have pulled the wool over the eyes of the voters, but some of his advisors may have, literally, put their hands over his eyes.

THEODORE
ROOSEVELT
26TH PRESIDENT
1901 – 1909

THEODORE ROOSEVELT

26th President ★ **1901–1909** ★ **Republican**

PENCIL SHARPENER

THEODORE "TEDDY" ROOSEVELT built the Panama Canal and won the Nobel Peace Prize. He was a trustbuster, Rough Rider, rancher, police commissioner, war cavalry hero, big game hunter, conservationist, and reformer. Somehow, the man who exhorted Americans to "carry a big stick" seems worthier of something more than being turned into a *plastic* pencil sharpener to keep all those little sticks at the ready.

> ...the man who exhorted Americans to "carry a big stick" seems worthier of something more than being turned into a plastic pencil sharpener...

Fear not, this plastic gizmo is one Teddy himself would have put through its paces. For starters, he wrote twenty-two books— military history, Western history, animal species, ranching—the list goes on. After leaving the White House, he wrote weekly editorials for the *Kansas City Star*, monthly articles for *Metropolitan Magazine*, African adventures for *Scribner's Magazine*, and essays for the *New York Times*.

Sum it all up and Teddy Roosevelt was the most prolific of presidents.

61

WILLIAM H. TAFT

27th President ★ 1909–1913 ★ Republican

CHRISTMAS TREE ORNAMENT

WILLIAM HOWARD "BIG BILL" TAFT was as warm and sweet, a friend said, as a saucepan of milk. But he pursued the presidency in large part at the urging his wife and brother—and it often left him in a state of depression.

As the blown-glass holiday ornament made by famed artist Christopher Radko in the 1990s, Taft recalls Christmas time, when sentiment can be tinged with family anxiety.

> ...to his more progressive critics, he was the man in the moon—blissfully ignorant of the world he looked down upon.

Taft plowed methodically toward reform, but to his more progressive critics, he was the man in the moon—blissfully ignorant of the world he looked down upon. There was some truth to that. Without guidance from his wife, who suffered a stroke, and his military aide, who died on the *Titanic*, Taft often had his head in the clouds, looking out for Halley's Comet, scheduled to whiz by in 1910.

WOODROW WILSON

28th President ★ **1913–1921** ★ **Democrat**

PIPE

ALL HE REALLY WANTED, claimed his supporters, was world peace. Certainly, if Woodrow Wilson had had any notion that the Treaty of Versailles would be followed by the Second World War, he'd have insisted that the delegates pass the peace pipe around.

This intricately carved walnut pipe depicting Wilson was probably made during the 1912 election. After being re-elected on a slogan of "He Kept Us Out of War," he got us into war. Then Wilson unveiled his grand vision for the League of Nations.

> "Woody," as some in the press unsuccessfully sought to nickname him, was a thickhead ...

Wilson was idealistically stubborn. Following a stroke, which Republican enemies falsely suggested had resulted in insanity, he refused any compromises regarding his League—membership in which Congress ultimately rejected. "Woody," as some in the press unsuccessfully sought to nickname him, was a thickhead who left many wondering what he was smoking.

65

WARREN G. HARDING

29th President ★ **1921–1923** ★ **Republican**

GOOD LUCK CHARM

WHEN SUNSHINE APPEARED at Warren Harding's inauguration, the press touted the mysterious "Harding luck." Soon enough, visitors to Washington, D.C., could take home their own bit of Harding luck, in the form of this massive "lucky penny" souvenir. Made in 1922, it was about twenty times the size of a Lincoln penny.

> When sunshine appeared at Warren Harding's inauguration, the press touted the mysterious "Harding luck."

At the start of 1923, another "good luck" souvenir penny of Harding was issued—but it was considerably smaller. Was luck running out for this genial president? Details began leaking out about corruption within his administration, and when Harding died suddenly, whispers of murder surrounded his death—which was actually a misdiagnosed heart attack.

During his funeral, Harding was often compared to Abraham Lincoln. But news of the corruption soon spread, increasingly tarnishing Harding's reputation. The Harding penny, once so gigantic, disappeared by 1924. And the little Lincoln penny has endured.

CALVIN COOLIDGE

30ᵗʰ President ★ **1923–1929** ★ **Republican**

DOLL

WHILE HE DID, INDEED, DEEPLY LOVE his two sons, it is hard to fathom a less likely president to provide cuddly childhood comfort than Calvin Coolidge. The expression on the Cal doll's face is enough to make a frightened child cry loudly.

Coolidge spoke with a thin, nasal Vermont twang that was not especially soothing. Luckily for Calvin "Silent Cal" Coolidge, this curious representation of him is not a ventriloquist doll. There are no strings to pull to hear Coolidge's most memorable words. In fact, he says nothing. (Ironically, he was the first president whose State of the Union address was broadcast on radio.) When a Washington socialite once bragged to Coolidge that she had made a bet that she could get him to say more than two words, he turned to her and cracked dryly, "You lose."

> The expression on the Cal doll's face is enough to make a frightened child cry loudly.

HERBERT HOOVER

31ˢᵗ President ★ 1929–1933 ★ Republican
LEMONADE PITCHER

HERBERT HOOVER'S SUCCESS AS CHIEF of global food relief after World War I would overflow even this lemonade pitcher of his head. Used to promote his presidential candidacy in 1928, this enormous pitcher was one of a limited edition made by the Hall China Company for the Patriotic Products Association in Philadelphia.

Before and after his presidency, Hoover was one of the twentieth century's most generous humanitarians. But that was hardly his popular image as president. In the midst of the Great Depression he resisted massive government rescue of the economy, and soon clusters of the dispossessed were living in shantytowns dubbed "Hoovervilles." Unfairly blamed for the depression, Hoover did the best he could with lemons, but no sweetener could remove the sourness the dispossessed felt toward him.

> Before and after his presidency, Hoover was one of the twentieth century's most generous humanitarians.

71

FRANKLIN D. ROOSEVELT

32ⁿᵈ President ★ **1933–1945** ★ **Democrat**

CLOCK

FRANKLIN D. ROOSEVELT'S TENURE was remarkable—an economic depression and international war both occurred on his watch. Yet many Americans would forever associate his entrance into the White House as those happy days that were here again: Prohibition was over, a fact celebrated by the happy bar scene on the face of this rare bronze clock.

Labor Secretary Frances Perkins also appears, echoing the hope that "old man Depression" would be wiped out by New Deal jobs. And presiding over it all with his jaunty grin was FDR himself—a man as remarkable as his era. Disabled by polio, elected to an unprecedented four terms, he served as president for twelve years. One wonders how the man, who became increasingly feeble, managed to survive so long. Perhaps it was his own private happy days in his private study—he made a wicked martini.

> **Prohibition was over, a fact celebrated by the happy bar scene on the face of this rare bronze clock.**

HARRY S. TRUMAN

33rd President ★ **1945–1953** ★ **Democrat**

BOTTLE STOPPER

BY THE TIME HARRY TRUMAN LEFT THE presidency, his approval ratings were abysmal. Only years later did America appreciate his steady leadership through the end of World War II and its aftermath.

The snappy little fellow from Missouri enjoyed nothing more than a game of poker over some bourbon and branch. In the Atomic Age, most men considered a stiff cocktail to be a birthright. It was perhaps no coincidence that the world leaders of that generation found themselves on liquor bottle stoppers. Around a globe still recovering from war, people could have a good laugh at their leaders before crying into their cups.

> The snappy little fellow from Missouri enjoyed nothing more than a game of poker over some bourbon and branch.

One of the few presidential heads produced in Europe, this cork-carved Truman bottle stopper was part of a series made in post-war West Germany—a pretty quick return on the investment of that Marshall Plan.

MADE IN GER

DWIGHT D. EISENHOWER

34ᵗʰ President ★ 1953–1961 ★ Republican

SHAVING MUG

DWIGHT D. EISENHOWER, Supreme Commander of the Allied Forces before becoming president, was always affectionately known simply as Ike. While this old-fashioned shaving mug might have held a lot of whipped soap at one time, the real man's cerebrum was far more complicated than he liked to suggest. He dealt with problems ranging from civil rights to Joe McCarthy, with wars Korean and Cold, and added Alaska and Hawaii to the United States.

Ike was a foursquare, red-blooded, middle-aged, middle-class, Midwestern moderate.

Ike was a foursquare, red-blooded, middle-aged, middle-class, Midwestern moderate. He was addicted to golf, dined on a tin television tray while watching westerns, pored through Zane Grey novels, and grilled his own steaks "Pittsburgh black-and-blue" style. The last president to be completely bald, he was not the sort to be caught lounging at Camp David (the presidential retreat that he named for his grandson) in need of a shave.

77

JOHN F. KENNEDY

35th President ★ 1961–1963 ★ Democrat

SALT AND PEPPER SET

HE WAS A CHARMING MASSACHUSETTS millionaire war hero with movie-star good looks who made women swoon. The youngest man elected president, John F. Kennedy could counterbalance the harshness of resolving the Cuban Missile Crisis with the hope of his Peace Corps.

The Camelot years of his short presidency converged with a booming middle class and the mass-manufacturing of cheaper products, and Kennedyiana hit the market with some force—dolls, whistles, wall hangings, bank busts, stickpins, Halloween masks, key chains, and hot plates.

The Camelot years of his short presidency converged with a booming middle class...

Still, no product better represents the two sides of Gemini Jack than this ceramic salt and pepper shaker set: The president pours salt and his famous rocking chair dispenses pepper. Indeed, it was one way to put the handsome man in the White House perpetually within reach of those American housewives who seemed most drawn to him.

LYNDON B. JOHNSON

36th President ★ **1963–1969** ★ **Democrat**

SHIRT HANGER

A COMPASSIONATE MAN who never forgot his experience as a teacher, Lyndon Johnson of Texas also had ruthless ambition and a larger-than-life personality. As John F. Kennedy's vice president, he completed his assassinated predecessor's administration and went on to win his own term in 1964.

As president, he created an unprecedented domestic agenda that included the Civil Rights Act and the Head Start program. But his Great Society was soon eclipsed by the escalation of the Vietnam War.

> ...their message to LBJ was dead serious: Hang it up, Mr. President.

Produced in the psychedelic sixties, this cardboard and plastic Johnson shirt hanger was part of a series made by Famous Faces, Inc., that also included film stars. Hippies, flower children, and war protestors may have draped their tie-dyed shirts on one of these figures in a bit of sartorial satire, but their message to LBJ was dead serious: Hang it up, Mr. President. He did, deciding not to run again in 1968.

80

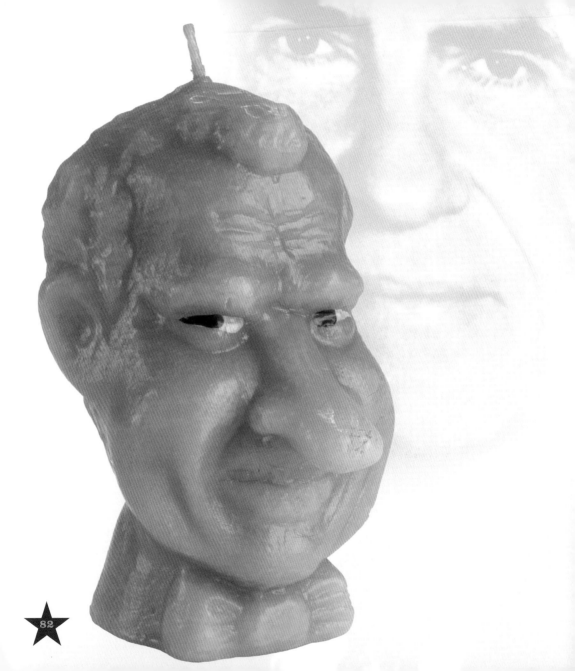

RICHARD NIXON

37ᵗʰ President ★ **1969–1974** ★ **Republican**

CANDLE

RICHARD NIXON BEGAN HIS PUBLIC CAREER as an anti-Communist congressman, and ended it as an elder statesman. But his presidential accomplishments were over-shadowed by his escalation of the Vietnam War he inherited from Lyndon Johnson and the Watergate scandal. He was the only president to resign.

He became one of the most caricatured presidents since Abraham Lincoln, vilified in cartoons and objects ranging from ping-pong paddles to showerheads. Yet through it all, he continued to work toward the détente he was determined to see through, building social and political bridges between the United States and China, and with the Soviet Union. It is no stretch of the imagination to say that Nixon burned the candle at both ends. And so, in that magnificent avocado green of the seventies, "Tricky Dick"—as his enemies called him—or RN, as he signed himself, is thus recalled in wax.

> It is no stretch of the imagination to say that Nixon burned the candle at both ends.

83

GERALD R. FORD

38th President ⭐ **1974–1977** ⭐ **Republican**

TEASPOON

THE TWENTY-NINE MONTHS of the Gerald Ford presidency may seem as small as this Bicentennial teaspoon depicting him in pewter. But he entered the White House faced with the task of healing the nation during a cynical and confusing time. The likeable persona of this Republican from Michigan reassured the public that integrity would be returned to the White House.

The most colorful event of Ford's era was the nation's celebration of two centuries of independence in July of 1976. Ford may have faced his own economic and energy crises, but after the assassinations of leaders, a divisive war, and political scandal, and before the omnipresence of terrorism and virulent partisanship, the Bicentennial Ford years seem a short, sweet spot in the mid-seventies, a spoonful of sugar between more bitter times.

> ...the Bicentennial Ford years seem a short, sweet spot in the mid-seventies...

84

JIMMY CARTER

BOTTLE OPENER

JIMMY CARTER'S BROAD, GRINNING TEETH were ubiquitous, appearing on everything from peanut wind-up toys to jewelry. But this vinyl "Happy Mouth" bottle opener is unique—Carter's teeth are missing. Manufactured by Thomas Premiums in Japan, the bottle opener fills Carter's mouth, and the back of the head comes off so one can retrieve the caps.

A Baptist deacon from Georgia, Carter pressed a vigorous agenda of global human rights and hammered out the Camp David Accords between Israel and Egypt.

Jimmy Carter's broad, grinning teeth were ubiquitous...

But he also faced an energy crisis, a nuclear reactor accident, inflation, recession, and the Iran hostage crisis.

Carter was even hurt politically by the exploits of his brother Billy, who had his own namesake beer. The brothers were as different as aluminum and glass—Billy Beer only came in cans, and the Carter opener only jimmied the caps off bottles.

RONALD REAGAN

40th President ★ **1981–1989** ★ **Republican**

TEAPOT

"**T**HE GIPPER," "TEFLON PRESIDENT," "Great Communicator"—Ronald Reagan had any number of nicknames during his two presidential terms. He was a master image-maker who began as a Hollywood actor, served as California's governor, and then landed in the White House.

Despite his rightwing politics, moving this ceramic teapot of Reagan, made by the Hall China Company, to the center of a negotiating table might practically forge global alliances. After he challenged Soviet President Mikhail Gorbachev to tear down the Berlin Wall, the two men signed the INF Treaty limiting nuclear weapons. But Reagan had a closer friendship with British Prime Minister Margaret Thatcher. One of the few faces welcomed in Ireland—his ancestral land—as well as in England, the Reagan on this teapot will long be recognized over a spot of tea in either country. Or in Russia, Poland, or East Berlin.

> He was a master image-maker who began as a Hollywood actor, served as California's gover-nor, and then landed in the White House.

GEORGE H.W. BUSH

41st President ★ **1989–1993** ★ **Republican**

KEYCHAIN

KEYED-UP, PERIPATETIC GEORGE BUSH golfed, fished, hunted, jogged, swam, bobsledded, played baseball, racquetball, horseshoes, and tennis—even after the discovery of a minor heart fibrillation.

In between dashing off his famous thank-you notes, the jittery gent jumped to open new doors for new leaders for his New World Order—Britain's John Major, Russia's Boris Yeltsin, Nicaragua's Violeta Chamorro—but jangled nerves with his Gulf War and Panama invasion. At home, the economy worsened while the "kinder, gentler" Houston Yankee signed the Americans with Disability Act.

> In-between dashing off his famous thank-you notes, the jittery gent jumped to open new doors for new leaders...

Satirized on the British TV show "Spitting Image," his caricature was merchandized as a salt shaker (with his wife as pepper) and a doggie squeeze doll. But the jingle of keys on the Bush keychain is far more in line with this hyperkinetic exec.

BILL CLINTON

42ⁿᵈ President **1993–2001** ★ **Democrat**

CORKSCREW

HIS ADMIRERS CALLED HIM "The Comeback Kid" and his detractors called him "Slick Willy," but there was no denying the statistics that emerged from Bill Clinton's presidency: the lowest inflation in thirty years, highest rate of home ownership in American history, and an unprecedented federal budget surplus.

The only Rhodes Scholar elected president, this Arkansas native was also the first since Andrew Johnson to endure impeachment. But he rose above bitter partisanship to lead bipartisan endeavors such as trade policies like NAFTA and GATT.

> Although some of these agreements would later prove controversial, they increased the flow of foreign products— including wine grapes . . .

Although some of these agreements would later prove controversial, they increased the flow of foreign products—including wine grapes—from many poorer nations into the United States. This didn't pop any corks in France, but it certainly opened the American market to less expensive wine. And a close look at the small print on this corkscrew practically screams open trade: "Made in Japan."

93

GEORGE W. BUSH

43rd President ⭐ **2001–** ⭐ **Republican**

JACK-IN-THE-BOX

DESPITE SERVING AS PRESIDENT during the September 11 terrorist attacks, George W. Bush was soon caricatured like every POTUS before him. Born and educated in New England, "W,"—as he's known—views himself as a Texan. And predictably enough, cartoonists most frequently depict him as a cowboy.

> So, just when least expected, "W" pops up with an element of "shock and awe."

Bush always rose to the challenge when others underestimated him. But certainly no political pundit could have predicted the results of the 2000 election when, for the second time in American history, a president's son won an election in the midst of disputed results. In fact, many insiders had thought his younger brother, Jeb, might be the son to follow their father into the White House.

So, just when least expected, "W" pops up with an element of shock and awe, thus making his depiction as a jack-in-the-box not really surprising at all.

ACKNOWLEDGMENTS

All objects are from the author's collection.

We acknowledge the following manufacturers:

p. 15, Falstaff Brewing Corporation; 16, Enesco; 19, Trenton Spirits, Ltd.; 20, Old English Staffordshire Ware, made especially for Ashlawn-Highland, Charlottesville, VA; 23, Rogers Manufacturing Co.; 24, Old Hickory Distilling Corporation; 27, White House Historical Association, Limited Edition 4434. The Franklin Mint © 1975; 45, © American Collectors Guild, The Historic Collection of American Presidents; 46, © 2002 Harmony Ball Pot Belly; 49, Spalding Molitor Titanium Power Golf Balls; 53, © 77FM; 63, Christopher Radko; 70, © Patriotic Products Association, Philadelphia, The Hall China Company #673 of a first and limited edition; 75, ACHATIT; 79, © Arrow NYC, 1962; 81, Famous Faces, Inc.; 82, Jack B. Nimble Candles & Such; 85, © Fort; 86, © 1976 Thomas Premiums, Ltd.; 89, The Hall China Company; 90, © Spitting Image Productions, Ltd., 1988; 95, The Presidential Jack-in-the-Box Collection ™, © 2001 DMA.

Presidential portraits courtesy Library of Congress, National Archives, Presidential Libraries, and the White House.